The
New Orleans
12 Days
of Christmas

Lisa Marie Brown
Illustrated by Sarah Cotton

PELICAN PUBLISHIN
New Orleans 2020

The word "Pelican" and the depiction of a pelican are trademarks of Arcadia Publishing Company Inc. and are registered in the U.S. Patent and Trademark Office.

Library of Congress Cataloging-in-Publication Data

Names: Brown, Lisa Marie, 1966- author. | Cotton, Sarah, 1991- illustrator.

Title: The New Orleans Twelve Days of Christmas / Lisa Marie Brown ; illustrated by Sarah Cotton.
Description: New Orleans : Pelican Publishing, 2020. | Summary: This variation of the folk song "The Twelve Days of Christmas" celebrates the uniqueness of Christmas in New Orleans.
Identifiers: LCCN 2018024106 | ISBN 9781455624539 (hardcover : alk. paper) | ISBN 9781455624546 (ebook)
Subjects: LCSH: Children's songs—United States—Texts. | Christmas music—Texts. | CYAC: New Orleans (La.)—Songs and music. | Christmas—Songs and music. | Christmas music. | Songs.
Classification: LCC PZ8.3.B81469 Ne 2019 | DDC 782.42 [E]—dc23
LC record available at https://lccn.loc.gov/2018024106

Printed in Malaysia
Published by Pelican Publishing
New Orleans, LA
www.pelicanpub.com

To my Ancestors who made New Orleans their home—L.M.B.

On the first day of Christmas,
my true love gave to me

moss hanging from an oak tree.

On the second day of Christmas,
my true love gave to me

two sweet pralines and
moss hanging from an oak tree.

On the third day of Christmas,
my true love gave to me

three beignets,
two sweet pralines, and
moss hanging from an oak tree.

On the fourth day of Christmas,
my true love gave to me
four riverboats,

three beignets,
two sweet pralines, and
moss hanging from an oak tree.

On the fifth day of Christmas,
my true love gave to me
five gold doubloons,
four riverboats,
three beignets,
two sweet pralines, and
moss hanging from an oak tree.

On the sixth day of Christmas,
my true love gave to me

six bowls of gumbo,
five gold doubloons,
four riverboats,
three beignets,
two sweet pralines, and
moss hanging from an oak tree.

On the seventh day of Christmas,
my true love gave to me
seven plates of red beans,
six bowls of gumbo,
five gold doubloons,
four riverboats,
three beignets,
two sweet pralines, and
moss hanging from an oak tree.

On the eighth day of Christmas,
my true love gave to me
eight jazz musicians,
seven plates of red beans,
six bowls of gumbo,
five gold doubloons,
four riverboats,
three beignets,
two sweet pralines, and
moss hanging from an oak tree.

On the ninth day of Christmas,
my true love gave to me

nine shotgun houses,
eight jazz musicians,
seven plates of red beans,
six bowls of gumbo,
five gold doubloons,

four riverboats,
three beignets,
two sweet pralines, and
moss hanging from an oak tree.

On the tenth day of Christmas, my true love gave to me

ten oyster po' boys,
nine shotgun houses,
eight jazz musicians,
seven plates of red beans,
six bowls of gumbo,
five gold doubloons,

four riverboats,
three beignets,
two sweet pralines, and
moss hanging from an oak tree.

On the eleventh day of Christmas,
my true love gave to me

eleven second-liners,
ten oyster po' boys,
nine shotgun houses,
eight jazz musicians,
seven plates of red beans,
six bowls of gumbo,
five gold doubloons,
four riverboats,
three beignets,
two sweet pralines, and
moss hanging from an oak tree.

On the twelfth day of Christmas,
my true love gave to me
twelve tasty king cakes,

eleven second-liners,
ten oyster po' boys,
nine shotgun
houses,

eight jazz musicians,
seven plates of red beans,
six bowls of gumbo,
five gold doubloons,

four riverboats,
three beignets,
two sweet pralines, and
moss hanging from an oak tree.

Author's Note

Are you more likely to see a partridge in a pear tree or moss hanging from an oak tree? Who wants to look at lords a-leaping when watching second-liners is more fun? Would you prefer drummers drumming or eating a king cake? Well, these are a few of the gifts in "The Twelve Days of Christmas," but with a New Orleans twist. The New Orleans retelling of the traditional carol provides a delightful way to pass a good time with Christmas gifts you really want. After Hurricane Katrina in 2005 almost threatened our way of life for future generations, I wanted to ensure that our heritage is never forgotten. I used a popular song to teach young readers about the people, food, and icons of New Orleans culture in a fun way.